FRAGMENTS

Shuvashree Chowdhury

First published in India in 2018 by CinnamonTeal Publishing

Copyright © 2018 Shuvashree Chowdhury

ISBN 978–93–87676–00–8

BISAC Code: POE000000/POETRY/General

Typesetting and Cover design: CinnamonTeal Design and Publishing

CinnamonTeal Publishing
an imprint of CinnamonTeal Design and Publishing
Plot No 16, Housing Board Colony
Gogol, Margao
Goa 403601 India
www.cinnamonteal.in

Praise for Shuvashree Chowdhury's debut novel, *Across Borders*

'A moving and evocative novel that vividly captures our past.'
— TIMERI N MURARI, novelist & playwright, recipient of the R K Narayan Award

'An urgent tale told with utter vividness. An important addition to the literatures from India's North-East and Bangladesh.'
— SUDEEP SEN, author of *Fractals: New & Selected Poems | Translations: 1980-2015*; *The HarperCollins Book of English Poetry* & *EroText*

'The book is unputdownable. How many people can write as powerfully as Shuvashree Chowdhury?'
— PRANAY GUPTE, journalist & author

'Across Borders holds you with its vivid descriptions and its delineation of characters. Moving across the important decades of our early independence, it tells stark and often poignant stories.'
— RUCHIR JOSHI, writer & columnist, *The Telegraph* (Kolkata)

'An engrossing storyteller .... The delineation of characters is superb, so true and real that they come to life. I was able to identify myself with many situations. I finished reading the novel in two straight sittings.'
— P V KRISHNAMOORTHY, (first) Director General, *Doordarshan*

'The author has surpassed herself in fleshing out the primary characters. But her strength lies in linguistic flair, especially in descriptive prose. There are myriad evocative turns of phrase throughout the novel, each a delicate brushstroke that adds luminosity to a master canvas. It is in these compelling details that Across Borders stands out as a commendable body of work, its vivid details evocatively blending history with fiction.'
— *The Telegraph*

For my mother, Mahamaya,
From whom I inherited poetry

Table of Contents

FRAGMENTS

Vision Statement

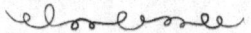

To create a picturesque,
Meaningful
And fragrant garden
Of thoughts and words
In my lifetime,
That will give wings to dreams
In the youth that find solace
On branches of my views
Even after my death:
To build a tomb
Over green thoughts
Of integrity
And a strong character
For themselves,
In my name.

—*Shuvashree*

A Poem

A propelling word and then a few lines
Spurting compelling thoughts in my mind,
I first mark them down at the nick of time
Lest they involuntarily leave me behind.

These lines delve into a maze of thoughts
That chase unconscious, unravelled tracks:
I then let myself get lost in their troughs—
They lead me to my core, to veiled grasslands.

I'm surprised by the intricacy of my soul
Whose thoughts I unconsciously abhorred,
Yet it was that momentous fleeing thought
That has led me to myself—otherwise lost.

From deep within the fissures of my mind—
A well of experience, emotions, wisdom arises:
Infusing a repertoire of words I've imbibed—
A poignant, myriad kaleidoscope I inscribe.

A Lonely Star

In life's long journey I needed a friend,
I looked in all directions—you let out your hand:
A life-saving shaft in a turbulent sea—
I grabbed it and held on as tight as can be.

Clinging to it I swam to the shore—
The crowd, the neon lights, scared me so;
I looked back to see the lean strong hand
But, lo and behold, it just did not show.

Seeing the men and women cheer me so
You thought I would let your hand go;
The men and women do not know my goals
But you my friend were the crutch of my soul.

The men and women who cheer me so
Only know the beauty at the fore,
They do not have time to look into the core—
Which my friend is what you alone know.

My heart and soul were yours to protect—
To safeguard from the feeling of unrest;
But you my friend would rather save a moth,
Brilliance of a butterfly could blind you thought.

Without the strength of your hand to shelter me—
Don't you see I am just a caterpillar on a tree?
Come my friend give me your hand once more,
Turn me into a butterfly with shine and lore.

Shuvashree Chowdhury

Wherever in the world I may fly or be,
Men and women will only behold me;
However, you my friend will only always see—
The brilliance that lies inside of me.

I am a lonely star don't you see—
Lost in a galaxy of revelry?
Come my friend out of a caterpillar set me free:
I'm a butterfly for the world to perceive!

A Handsome Couple

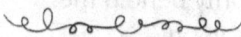

You said you loved me—but you lied,
I was just an object in your eyes;
An item to flaunt in the public eye,
To boost your ego, bring you into limelight.

My foolish heart—believed your words,
It longed to be loved, it longed to be hugged:
Believing you would love me forever
I bartered my love for your wandering lust.

You treated me well, you handled me right—
I was a naive princess in your eyes;
You gifted me well, dined me in style,
The wine for sure blinded my trusting sight.

Just when I was sure we could last forever,
You told me I was not the only one dear:
That there were others your heart desired—
Who gave themselves to you without a tremor.

I had given you my heart, bequeathed my soul,
So my foolish heart passed all this off as a joke:
Your passionate kisses had blinded me so—
How could you ever love anyone more?

My light and shine I had passed on to you,
You were now at the centre of the world:
Robbing my light—you now shone bright,
While I was happy to glow in your light.

Shuvashree Chowdhury

Then one fine day in front of my eyes—
What do I see by the shimmering seaside?
A man in black, the woman in white:
You the man, the woman—of whom you had lied!

Walking up to you in the wind and the surf—
I rolled into my voice an impeccable calm,
"You make a handsome couple" I said, flashing my best smile:
My eyes—they stung, my heart burnt amber in the cool night.

A Green Stretch

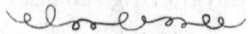

In a pine wood with winding mud-tracks—
There's green stretches where cows graze,
The breeze here bounces off lashing waves
As it embalms the scent of the sea in haste.

It's few hours' drive out of the city here—
A weekend getaway, a charming locale;
Amidst childhood friends I feel safe now
As no pretence I need to convey all's well.

The chalet is empty, the others are out—
I opted for a rendezvous with my mind;
It's been so long since I could spare time
To romance emotions flurried over time.

Moonlight on my face, I'm awake in bed
As I listen to the leaves rustle in the wind,
Over the gurgle of the sea rough at night
I still hear the clamour of thoughts within.

My mind discerns what it must do now
But my heart puts up a stiff, strong fight,
Between the two I am squashed in pain—
Sitting on a bed of arrows life provides.

Injured, the heart never loses its yearn—
However much the cognizance of strife,
Till it's crushed to the very core by fraud—
Defeating, eradicating, its trust in mankind.

Shuvashree Chowdhury

I must rise over din that crushes humanity,
Listen to the sound of the sea and of life,
I must heal now—raise my soul from ashes,
As to live without trust would mean I'd die!

I doze off, my mind exhausted from combat,
Tired of chiding my heart ever ready to trust:
I open my eyes to bright sunlight on my face—
I know I'll upkeep faith in humanity—not doubt!

Your Hidden Face

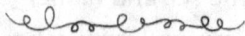

In the rain on leaves I see your face—
Shapeless, green and tenderly faint,
Floating in my memory as in a haze,
Yet your soul I brazenly embraced.

You speak to me as soft as a breeze—
Caressing my face, tender on my skin;
Drops of rain fall steady on the roof
As loud as your unspeaking words do.

Chirping of a range of birds that abound,
Trying to drown the sound of rain's fall
That drips steady, drop by drop on walls:
But I hear dribs—pure as I do your voice.

Dark swimming clouds slowly waft by
Clearing a lighted spectrum in the sky,
As a band of birds fly past a lit cosmos
Drawing attention to your smiling face.

Now I see your face distinctly bright—
The one hidden so long from my sight;
It is the one I speak to in my dreams—
My imagination now has your sheen!

Shuvashree Chowdhury

Imagination of Love

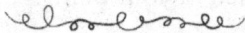

"I love you as certain dark things are to be loved,
in secret, between the shadow and the soul."—Pablo Neruda.

Why is it that I miss you so—only
Days since you're at another shore!
Why am I not able to make you see
You've begun to mean the world to me?

Why does it not matter how you feel
So long as my heart can intone steadily?
After long I now feel light and cheery—
Of my loneliness I've learnt to be free.

Thinking of 'us' now makes me smile
As in my imagination we have a life,
In which we wake together at dawn—
Each of us to our private thoughts.

Over tea, as we overlook the blue sea,
From our balcony amidst tall trees;
We see the sun beaming cheerily—
Caressing the sea—gurgling shyly.

It's as I giggled in your arms last night
When teasingly you made love to me:
You never cease to make me smile
Which in turn gives you a steady high.

In your mind, you also play this scene
Where you make love to me tender, sweet.

Though in real life we're as yet to meet,
I can now feel every inch of your being.

Imagination is like the gleam of the sun
That permeates where nothing else can:
It warms or scorches us with its intense rays,
Shielding us from life's cruel, virulent haze.

Shuvashree Chowdhury

The Rain Song

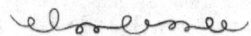

Sitting on my balcony
I watch the green sight:
The top of trees quiver,
Their leaves drip light.

The sky dark as night
Yet with hints of light;
Crows hop restlessly
On branches astride.

Thunder rips my soul,
Light dazzles my sight
As sound of steady rain
Soaks my heart's quiet.

Music playing indoors
Pervades my senses—
Lyrics soft and tender
As if rain in my mind.

Amidst gleams of light
Thunder roaring aloud,
I hear soft rain on leaves
Singing a ballad of my life.

Cold at Your Door

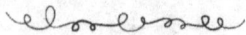

"Oft expectation fails, and most oft there where most it promises."
William Shakespeare —'All's Well That Ends Well.'

All I wanted from you is a little shade—
A little shelter from the rain I desired;
Cover from the torrential pour outside,
A safe haven is all my soul considered.

It wasn't your heart I wanted for myself,
Neither a space in your house did I ask;
Refuge from the torrent is all I coveted
Till I could find my own bearing upright.

You then indicated an illusionary space—
Permitted me a canopy on your porch;
But my heart tripped in the torrential rain
So you left me outside—cold in the dark.

Amassing my self-esteem from your egress
I walked out bare, abashed, a mere wobble—
Drenched, in public view I stood vulnerable:
True love came by—straddled me in its lurch!

Shuvashree Chowdhury

Amidst the Vines

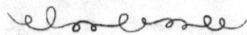

Lonely I stood amidst the vines
In a pall of temerity, as standby;
You came strolling by the woods
In search of harmony and quiet.

In bloom, concealed from view
I was timid to step into public eye,
As for long I was veiled from sight—
Lighting a green stage as floodlight.

As visible, I might gleam as sunshine,
Blind viewers from seeing starlight—
Of skills he's rehearsed a lifetime,
Thus I hesitated to show my glow.

But you caught a glint of my light,
Acknowledged I had my own shine
Over merely illuminating the stage—
Thus recouped me with flashlight.

A Literary Crush

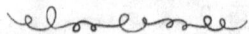

First it was your lyrical words I met,
Then it was your enchanting thoughts;
Through them different worlds I viewed—
My arms tucked into yours I walked.

It kept raining in that world we trooped
As drenched through our skins we were,
Yet I did not feel the moist on my skin
As your magical words warmed my heart.

I traversed with you through hills and plain—
My hand securely clasped in yours;
You led me through wind and snow alike,
Through rain that never left our side.

In my heart I knew you so well by now,
Even though we were as yet to meet;
Your soul had reached out to touch mine
As words travel where none can reach.

So when you opened your door that night,
My soul walked right into your arms;
Though we looked on as strangers do—
Our hearts melted effortlessly into one.

The wine you poured warmed my blood
Yet a chill ran down my heart and spine;
Worried I was you could hear my heartbeat
As loud as thunder of that clammy night.

Shuvashree Chowdhury

Though I kept rambling incessantly
Over the book release and then dinner,
I wish I could bring myself to tell you
A mere hug could make me steadier.

As you walked me home in the chill—
A good distance we kept in our strides;
I spoke ceaselessly till we reached my gate
But nothing of what went on in my mind.

This meeting, I dreamt after reading your book
As I fell asleep with it covering my brazen heart;
But not before you'd kissed my soul with steady lips—
After which I melted into the warmth of your arms!

Love at First Sight

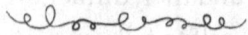

I searched the world that I may find
A love that is pure and truly divine,
That which I could say was only mine—
Comforting me from squall and strife.

In my dreams love had no face—
It was an illusion I earnestly chased;
A complex maze into which I raced,
With my perceptions—an image I traced.

Into that image I breathed form and life—
My hearts desires and longings to abide;
When it took the effigy I inscribed
I mistook it for love at first sight.

With the passage of time, I realized
The qualities I had myself surmised
Into the image I had infused with life—
In a deluge began to be refused.

In my mind, I had created this form
With which my heart keenly fell in love,
Is it then that I might say love is blind
Or is it the reflection of my own light!

When I accept the worth of the one I love
By acknowledging he is unique and one,
Then can I be blessed with lasting love—
A love that is pure and true in every form!

Shuvashree Chowdhury

The Colours of my Passion

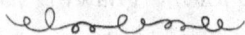

I dialled your number so many a times—
Love, my love, why wouldn't you reply?
It drove me crazy, it drove me wild
Knowing you were at the end of the line.

You had said I was not good for you
Cause in my rage I had abused you,
But you know Darling, that it is true—
I am jealous of anyone else near you.

But now that you've let down your guard
And let me back again into your heart,
Wait till I prove to you, oh my love—
The colour of my passion is not all green!

I wait in anticipation once more on the road
For you to pick me up as usual at my door;
We drive away into the sunset once more—
Heart-to-heart, soul-to-soul, sealed at the core.

As we sit down cosily by our favourite shore—
My passion is brighter than the setting suns glow;
You kiss me tender—you kiss me so soft,
Igniting the cinders of your passion once more.

Then unable to withstand the longing any more
We mindlessly devour each other by the shore;
The sky and sea—mute spectators to our spree
As we cling together, like wet sand to our feet.

How did you think you could just let me go—
The passionate longing for me, gnawing you so!
As you gently lower your head to taste my peak—
A meteor, I shatter into a thousand stars in ecstasy.

The myriad colours of my passion, love do you see—
Passing through the prism that is me: Purple, Orange,
Vermilion, Gold—Green is not the only colour it knows:
Darling don't you see—your light defines the hues in me!

Shuvashree Chowdhury

On the Horizon

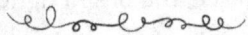

I step out onto the road once more
To drive away into the setting suns glow,
Keeping the sea to the left side of me
We head to the place where we first meet.

The cobalt blue sea flowing alongside me
Emanates the hue—reflecting the sky true;
The dark cloud overcast sky makes the boats pry—
As the moist sea breeze makes love to me serene.

En route we alight for coffee and a bite,
Ducks and rabbits we feed—our minds casual and free;
You look tenderly at me, breaking through my reverie—
I appear serene, in spite of the wind tossing me.

We then drive through the gate, to a garden ablaze
With tiny twinkling lights—my heart setting astride;
By now my passion strong and deliriously true—
Over my duty and vows falling through.

We walk down the dim, sandy shore—
The warm moonlight setting our hearts aglow;
Soft waves breaking on a pristine, secluded coast—
Louder than my heart and conscious in a row.

Surf encircling our feet, your arms engulfing me—
You softly kiss my lips, as moonlight kisses the sea's tip;
We gently descend on the shore—by now our passions' a roar,
Sand cradling me deep, a blanket of stars covering us steep.

My passion now engulfing me, I look for the horizon in me—
Looking back can I still see, the bright lights cajoling me?
I then let myself go, knowing for sure I can return once more,
To the lights—my vows beckoning me: I'm not far gone you see!

Shuvashree Chowdhury

Blinded in Love

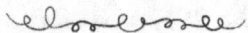

I don't know where, I don't know how,
I just fell in love somehow;
Lord my God, can you vividly see
What in him do I honestly see!

Is it his sense of humour that propels me,
Or is it his smile that magnetizes me?
Am I sold to his wit my lord,
Or is it his touch to which I am lost?

Is it his words that are tender and sweet,
Or is it his gestures that fascinate me?
Lord my God can you tell me now—
Is it his gaze that turns me on somehow!

Someday when I can impartially see—
Is when this love is no longer in me:
Till the love in my heart resides so deep,
Blinded in love I might forever be!

Passion

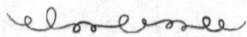

It strikes, ignites you,
Seeps you, fuels you,
Outwits, propels you,
Blinds you, scalds you.

A splinter traces you—
Splits you, probes you.
The flame engulfs you—
Nuzzles, caresses you.

As it crushes you down—
Intimately it shocks you,
Rocks you, frenzies you,
Melts you, trickles you.

Burning out inside you,
Exuding, drenching you—
Diffusing, satiating you:
Leaving you cold to touch.

Shuvashree Chowdhury

Long Distance Love

Driving in through the iron gates—
At a beautiful garden—I gaze;
Bluebells swaying on either side,
A humming bird chirping to my right.

Waiting in the car for you to check us in—
My heart in my mouth, I sadly think:
A great job opportunity though it is,
Can our love survive this distant stint?

Tomorrow you will have to go away,
Today is all we have to embrace;
As you may not return before long,
We have to make the most of today.

The Daisies, Tulips, Carnations, all
Are mute spectators to my aching heart,
For how do I just let you go away—
Why can't we together, forever stay?

Quietly we now sit by the fire place:
My grieving heart why can't it just wait?
Let me enjoy the warmth of your embrace—
For tomorrow is as yet far away!

A Shooting Star

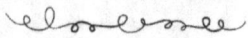

As she walked into the hall that night
She was the cynosure of everyone's eyes,
With elegance and poise she passed on by
Introduced to all the guests in her stride.

Her brown hair cascading to her waist,
Peaches-crème skin illuminating her face;
Tall and slender was her popular frame,
A disarming smile and poise she displayed.

Men, they looked at her with a sigh—
Transported now to a different, new high:
Drowning themselves in her deep brown eyes
As she sensuously smiled in the dim light.

Women looked at her at first in awe
But soon their insecurities did them devour,
Thus unable to return her beaming smile
They greeted her with nods that were snide.

The celebration by now was in full swing—
People immersed in the food and drinks;
Music setting the mood for dancing,
People lowering their guard in carousing.

The men on that carefree jovial night—
On the splendour of the film star feasted their eyes,
Imagining they could make her their bride
For their own partners—did far from shine bright.

Shuvashree Chowdhury

Admiring the brilliance of a shooting star is all right
So long as you value the real star by your side:
Cause a meteor is just an amazing streak of light—
Caused by tiny bits of rock and dust, in sight.

The Perfect Woman

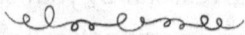

Wasn't it till last night that we were friends,
Lovers, partners and all relations else?
But today is the beginning to the end
As now we will remain at our own ends.

Last night you told me there's someone new—
How can I tolerate this over all else I do?
Weren't we destined to be together till the end—
Wonder what really happened to us then!

You told me I wasn't woman enough for you
Cause I talked too much and was egotistic too;
Affectionate and warm I wasn't to you,
In addition to that—always nagging you.

You said I ought to be polite, adjust with you,
Be supportive, not draw comparisons to you;
I should listen without much debate too
And remain calm, while totally trusting you.

I don't fit into the groove of a 'perfect woman'
For I flare at the slightest provocation;
Arguments are an integral part of my psyche,
Over and above—I incessantly talk nonsense.

A man, you said, there's out there for me
But you certainly aren't meant for me,
So I may settle with any other man I want—
You've found the woman you truly love.

Shuvashree Chowdhury

I know what you said of me is so untrue—
My jealousy often makes me a stranger to you;
Of another woman you were seeing I knew
Yet I prayed and hoped this wasn't true!

Couldn't you leave me with my dignity intact?
Excuses I didn't need, of your disloyalty I knew:
Killing my naive spirit was brutally cruel—
How can I overcome this degradation so crude!

The real test of love is tolerance of weaknesses,
For it doesn't take love to accept solidity and talents:
I'm not the 'perfect woman' you said, didn't you—
A 'perfect woman' accepts flaws—as I did all yours!

Set me Free

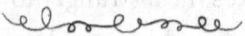

Just love me as I am
And let me love you as I can,
For only when I am really me
Can I truly be part of a—'we'

Just allow me to be free
That I can first value the—'me':
Then as I learn to love myself
I will love you like no one else.

Let me spread my wings
Like a bird soaring in spring,
See what joy I then bring
To our lives—like bells ring!

Don't try to pin me down,
Just let me fly in the clouds:
After I have roamed the world—
On your shoulder I will perch.

My colours illuminating your world,
A halo around your self-worth;
In your light I will now brightly shine
As the moon reflects the sun's light!

Shuvashree Chowdhury

Together for a Day

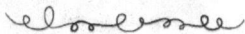

As we stood forlorn by the sea shore—
Lost in our private thoughts galore,
The waves crashed loudly on the shore
Reminding us we would be together no more.

Tomorrow will decide our love's destiny—
A love that once was but can no more be:
Since we have come a long, long way ahead,
Somehow leaving far behind our affections.

As the judge unties our marriage vows
Setting us free from the clutches of doubt,
No longer will we be together from now—
Yet can we not remain friends somehow?

Tomorrow is still another day—faraway,
Today is what we have together to retain:
Deciding to be the 'perfect couple' for today
In the hope this memory will forever stay!

Leaving our inhibitions behind this day—
We drive away to that familiar place:
For one last time we defy our fate,
To change what has now become hate.

The room is cosy, warm and true—
It's our passion that rings fake, untrue:
Just once more can't we honestly be
Happy—like we once used to be!

A Symphony

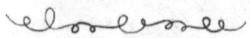

What is it that we want in our lives—
Is it a human love or a love truly divine?
A love that will see us through thick and thin
Or a love that throws all caution to the wind?

Do we want love to be a harmonious song
Calmly serenading us till dusk—from life's dawn?
Or do we want it to be a rock concert lifelong—
Perhaps we'd prefer an orchestra to play along?

Do we want love to be a canoe riding the waves—
Tossed excitingly in a turbulent sea full of rage?
Or we'd want it to be a boat anchored safe and secure—
Watching life go by, from the moonlit sandy shore?

Thrills and excitement in life are fleetingly transient—
That which survives the long haul is worthy and real,
Then why for ephemeral joys do we plunge into sea—
Colourful, frisky, though everything in it seems to be?

The thrills of going to sea could drown us painfully—
Should we then not be anchored to relationships dutifully:
Composing a Symphony of myriad hues and notes—
Finding in it everlasting peace, love, comfort and hope!

Shuvashree Chowdhury

View from my Balcony

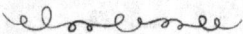

Since a child I loved to watch—
From my balcony the world go past:
Then it was at work I quietly drew
Sketches of men and women I knew.

An airline stint gave me a bird's eye view,
Then the career in retail a ringside view;
But it was the brief head-hunting stint
That gave me insight to what lay within.

Today, I still curiously view the world—
Of caprices of existences I encounter:
As mute or astute—I get a myriad view
Of human psyche rich, varied and true.

Homeward, on a Dream Trail

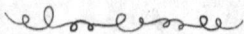

The narrow winding mud road
Ran into the deep green woods,
Even as I looked at it enchanted—
I rushed by on tracks by the brook.

Where might the road have lead me—
How I wish I had followed its trail:
Perhaps to a stream gurgling by hills
So I'd stretch on nature's green stage.

I'd watch the birds regale a blue sky
Forming patterns only I can ascribe;
The sun beaming, guiding their spree—
Through green trees I'd watch its rays.

A white rabbit might hop over to me
Distinct amidst lilacs and blue daffodils,
To offer his hand to any aid I might need
In the solitude of his home that's exquisite.

My face sprinkled by a waterfall I'd reply:
"No, I'm not lost, I have just found a home
As none I've lived in; like no friend nor joy—
Which, would you not allow me to enjoy!"

He'd accept, yet I'd chug by on steel tracks,
Never this narrow, winding track to traverse:
In returning to my world—to reality and life
At home—where there's struggle, also Hope.

Shuvashree Chowdhury

Rewinding Life

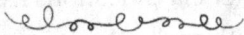

Sitting at the rooftop coffee shop,
People around us we silently watch:
Are they all just as happy as us
In sharing their life over coffee thus?

A lifetime nearly since we are friends,
Though we now reside at different ends;
Having come to our hometown now
Allows us to catch up on life somehow.

"Would you want to live life over again,"
Sipping my mint ice-tea I wistfully ask,
"In going back to college do you think—
We could once again bring back that zing?"

Digging into her blueberry muffin she sighs,
"Ah! Those fancy-free days, multiple-date nights,
When classes we missed for movies and pubs—
Wouldn't we do anything to get them back!"

Life is now monotonous and not much fun—
Duties, responsibilities, we cannot shun:
Wife, mother, daughter, we're all at once;
Isn't being a boss the most daunting one!

After a sip of her café latte she ruefully smiles,
"Ah! The cute guy with the crush on you so high..."
"One who chased me in and out of class," I reply,
"Doesn't it all now seem so much of the past!"

It's with close friends like us we can really be,
Only 'me'—from all other classifications free;
Sharing our failings with each other as now—
We step out of playing superwomen somehow!

As the guys who once chased us all over town,
Married to us—chase flourishing careers now;
Children too once grown, from home will leave—
Then on our concrete friendship may we lean.

Life's road can often be steep and uphill—
Holding each other's hands we'll trudge on still;
So then why wouldn't we always truly remain,
Cheerful and carefree—as we once used to be!

Shuvashree Chowdhury

My Dream Home

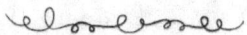

In the deep woods by the brook—
Amidst lilacs, parrots in the bush,
Where Mynas chirp, Cranes hop,
Is our cabin of bricks and wood.

A tiny bridge over the clear creek—
Pretty in yellow, green, cheery in look:
You cross it as you would a gateway,
Step into a garden our lodge embraces.

Up the stairs, made of trunks from the woods,
Atop a tree—my home is perched in its nook.
Over the fireplace lie open two poetry books
By a bottle of red wine two stem-glasses stand.

The wine awaits us—from an evening walk
Through winding tracks around a waterfall,
Over trails on which squirrels cross our path
But the woodpeckers don't stop to stare at us.

The setting sun is warm and tender on our skin,
In pink, orange, gold—hues of love, it streams;
As we stride cosily hand-in-hand in the woods
Flushed from yearning—of a love that soothes!

Truly at Home

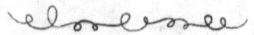

Durga Puja is soon coming along,
Bringing with it both cheer and song;
My heart's been craving for so long,
For the festivities: I've been forlorn!

New clothes I'll wear on all four days—
Changing twice, maybe thrice a day;
With family and friends I'll hang out,
Visiting pandals—mostly eating out.

The sound of *dhaak* awakening in me—
Reverence for the strength of Ma Chandi:
With the smell of *dhuno* through my senses,
Wafting in through the *dhunuchi* dances.

Shakha, paula, kangan adorning my wrists,
With vermilion my long hair I will now rift;
Bangla rock bands and Rabindra Sangeet
Will be the music to which I'll retreat.

Mughlai parathas, tele bhaja and *kathi rolls*
Will be staples, along with the *khichuri bhog*;
The *mahabhoj* I might have at my puja pandal
But it's the Chelo Kebab of Petercat I'll evoke.

Kishore Kumar, Hemanta Mukherjee, Manna Dey
Will be the backdrop singers when pandals I parade;
Sandhya, Arati Mukhopadhyay and others shall sing—
Traditions of the true Bengali spirit in me now to ring.

Shuvashree Chowdhury

They'll soon be here, those happy Puja days now
As I'll again be so much a part of my hometown:
Kolkata has only and always meant home to me—
Where Ma Durga is truly at home, just like me!

The Essence of Your Hand

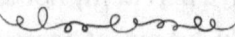

Dad, you taught me right from wrong,
Always filled my lips with joyous song;
Whenever I slipped you held my hand—
Helping me leave imprints in the sand.

I sought in you strength and support
When on others I could not depend:
My life was often turbulent and blue—
But you helped me sail right through.

My eyes and smile I inherited from you—
Always, forever reminding others of you.
But I was forever only a little girl to you
Whose hand you held tight right through.

In the evenings opening the doors to you,
Ensured—with chocolates you walked through;
Your charming warmth coming home with you—
Picking me up, you hugged me close to you.

In life's long journey I keep looking for you—
In whom do you reside so I may find you?
Now that you're gone all that's always there,
Is the essence of your firm, supportive hand.

Shuvashree Chowdhury

The Guiding Star

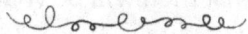

Whenever I needed you, you were there
Whether or not I've asked for your hand;
You have always been the Guiding Star—
Shining on me from wherever you are.

You always urged me to go that extra mile
To ensure my future is wrapped in a smile;
Who I am today, is because you were there—
Nudging me, when my mind wasn't made up.

After often prodding me—right over the top,
You ensured you were there to cushion my fall:
If it had not been for your firm, propelling hand—
As an oyster I might have remained in my shell.

"One's work is what will count," you always said,
"Beauty regimes, fashion, can be done without."
You'd say to me, "Never ever neglect your duties—
Good things will then come to you automatically."

Every time in life's race I felt I couldn't carry on—
Holding my hand, alongside me you ran along:
When the baton in exasperation I've dropped,
Picking it up, you've ensured I just did not stop.

Integrity, strength, and values you inculcated in me;
Also a sense of duty, confidence, and self-discipline:
Whenever in life's journey I might begin to slip,
It's your teachings every time I will mentally flip.

All your efforts Mother, may they not go in vain,
My success in life, is what then will be your gain.
Truly fortunate I have been throughout my life—
An excellent coach, and role model in you to find.

Shuvashree Chowdhury

The Prism

At times, short verses I write
To capture momentous thoughts;
At others, to freeze what I just saw
I click photographs that could say it all.
A random sketch I might make on paper
As a maze of contradictory fleeting thoughts:
To it I might add brush strokes of varied colour
That reflects light through the prism of my heart.
I feel compelled to express myself in sundry form
So as to deter my mind and my soul from steady rot.
I keep flowing like a rolling stone—so I gather no moss.

To Fly

I let go of the small things—
They only weigh me out,
I let go of restricting values
That pin my wings down.

I let go of negative people
Who leave a toxic residue,
I let go of what defines me—
Embrace an emancipated view.

I let go of curbing inhibitions
To fly high up into the clouds:
I watch my spirit circle and soar—
And feel my heart tenderly glow.

Shuvashree Chowdhury

Unaccompanied

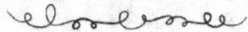

At times I have so much to say,
At other times nothing at all.

Sometimes I feel one with the world,
Often from outside I view the world.

At times I want to be amidst people,
Quite often, just alone with my thoughts.

However in life I equate with the world—
I know, one day—Alone—I must depart!

Firmly I Stood

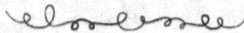

A moonless night it was—
Stars were shining bright,
Calm and quiet was the sea
As the waves lashed its sides.

Foam caressing my feet I stood
As the ground under me sank,
While the waves returning to sea
Washed away sand below my feet.

Life at times gently caresses my feet,
Also rudely pulls away the lush carpet:
I dug my feet into a slip, sliding ground—
Awaiting waves to return, bringing sand.

Shuvashree Chowdhury

As I Traverse

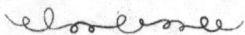

Green, green, green, is all I can see
As I slice through the face of diversity:
I'm travelling south to north of India—
It's a land enigmatic to say the least!

Tall white birds fly low over lush grass
That twinkles delightfully in the sunlight,
As shimmering rivulets and lakes gush
Below pretty bridges on which tracks run.

Clusters of coloured graves with crucifixes
Stand embedded on earth amid palm groves;
As tall, cheerful, deity engraved temples stand
With colourful idols carved large on pink walls.

Amid ceaseless stretches of lush brown fields
Haystacks stand as clusters of village huts,
While on trees amidst them white birds fly
Over sunburnt men, women, bent at work.

My eyes glued to the sights from my train berth,
As soft music plays into my ears from an IPod:
I concede to culture so diverse, south to north—
On a landscape distinctly changing hue and tone.

The Pearl

Sitting quietly by the shore—
Basking in the setting sun's glow,
The sand warm between my toes,
I search for myself once more.

Lost in this world I am—
Among my identities trapped:
Like a tiny spec of sand
Within an oyster lying entrapped.

As wife, daughter and colleague, I am
In a tiny spec of sand compressed,
In an oyster of womanhood encased—
Struggling to fit the mould with grace.

Water slowly seeping into the oyster,
Cradling the sand tenderly thereafter—
Is like love percolating into my life:
My identities somehow binding tight.

With time, it will be all this love—
Like water enclosing a spec of sand,
That will turn me into a shining Pearl
Of the garland of womanhood of the world.

An Exemplary Woman

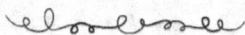

Smart, elegant, and beautiful,
At times volatile, but never spiteful;
Always proactive and respectful
To the point of self-effacement,
From a denial of personal fulfilment.

A doting and loving wife; but
It's as a mother her qualities shine:
As over and above attention she lavishes,
A habit of reading she encompasses;
The verbal rod to discipline she aptly uses.

Her duties as daughter-in-law, sister-in-law,
Of every other distant relation, she abides—
At the cost of her own desires, friends,
Even her personal space and time:
'An exemplary woman'—ironically she defines!

The Mask I Wear

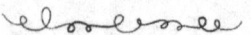

So much is bottled up within me—
Struggling to erupt, forcing to be free;
So much I hold with clenched teeth,
Screaming it out would liberate me.

Why is it, that I cannot break free
From the shackles that bind me?
Am I a prisoner of my own thoughts—
I am breaking within, let me out!

What is it that chokes my voice—
Bottling my tears in a tight vial?
Why does my face seem like a mask,
Hiding what is behind to unmask?

Why can't I beat the fear engulfing me
To allow people to look inside me?
Am I afraid they will not accept me—
Ridiculing the weakness they see in me!

It's only when I can shout out aloud,
Open the doors of my heart to let it all out;
Pull the mask off my vulnerable soul:
From the fragility strength will emerge!

Shuvashree Chowdhury

Crossroads

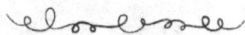

For long I waited to get a response,
A hope in my heart I silently nursed;
A dream, I earnestly and joyously cherished—
One day I would have my wishes fulfilled.

I put in all the efforts that I might—
With fervour I pursued my goals astride:
Along the way I neglected many other sights
Cause I was so focused on getting it right.

On the way disappointments did come,
When I thought my goal was out of sight:
It was then that I looked up to God—
A prayer in my heart—to light my path!

Today as I stand in the crossroads of life—
Wondering which road my life will ignite:
The path to my right seems so uphill,
The one to the left looks easy but so still!

The road in front may take me too far off,
One behind I might mistakenly leave behind!
How do I discern which road I need to take
To achieve my goals—my dreams to partake?

What if in the sole quest for my preferred road—
I'm so far gone, that all other paths close?
Will I then be happy—that I tried and lost
Or will I become despondent to have lost it all?

Let it Go

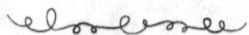

Acquaintances are aplenty,
True friends so few;
Loyalty is negligent,
Hypocrisy is widely strewn.

I'll let go off the duplicity
Of those supposedly friends—now untrue,
And embrace an emancipated view
To those I considered strangers, anew.

So if you should find that you're
From my friendship unexpectedly removed:
It's so I may clear convoluted emotional space—
Fill it with positivity, love of strangers too.

Shuvashree Chowdhury

A Sunshine

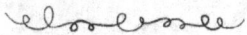

From my bed I saw the pale light—
An orange, purple, yellow sight:
Darkness below the shades was thick—
The sky merging with the sea at night.

Slowly from the light there arose,
Distinct from the myriad hues—
An orange ball of bursting light
Illuminating nearly half the world.

As I gazed awestruck by the sight
The ball turned yellow—lit the sky,
The sea shimmering with this light—
Gurgling aloud, slowly went quiet.

The wind on my cheeks moist, cool—
I watched sunlight fill up my room;
The birds fell silent—tired of chirping,
As the world gently began its song.

It was the beginning of a new day—
The genesis of a new phase today:
With this light of renewed hope—
A new life I'll lovingly, gently grope.

The past is no longer in my control
So the present I joyously behold:
With joy and love I embrace today—
As a beautiful future for me enfolds.

A New Life

There comes a time in your life
When you have to leave the past behind,
Move onto what's new and bright—
For only then a new life you'll inscribe.
It's time to embrace new friends
Who open up their lives to let you step in
And leave those who've shut their hearts,
Carry along those who've never left your side
Whether you're a success or failure in life.
True friends know how hard you've tried
To scale every rung that you've climbed,
After falling on your face quite often,
While good luck they've been given.
It is painful, but isn't it true—
You outgrow close relationships
And friendships that were once pure,
Just as you do clothes and shoes too!
Then why do I keep holding on
To the past, that's embedded in my heart:
Not allowing new relations to flourish—
In fear they'd not match what's lost and gone!

Shuvashree Chowdhury

Hide N Seek

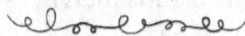

Waves softly breaking on the sea shore,
Sitting in the full moon's orange glow—
Feeling the cool sand between my toes,
Silently I wonder on life once more.

Another year has briskly gone by
Like quick sand in a dessert night,
Pulling me into the depths of time—
My head barely out of the earth's line.

Ever since I was a little girl, I'd become
Excited when my birthday came along,
Knowing that the next year would be
Closer to the finish, of life's marathon.

Now with the completion of another lap
When my birthday comes back—
Life's fatigue I invariably shirk away,
Like a girl—once again to enjoy the day.

Lost in these thoughts while I was—
The glowing moon just disappeared;
Looking up, when I couldn't see its glow,
A dejection crept into my soul.

Closing my eyes I made a sincere wish,
Opening them—that wish had fulfilled:
The moon was in its glorious glow—
Peeking at me with the clouds below.

Hide n Seek it was playing with me—
Skirting in and out of the clouds merrily:
Just as happiness has always been
Playing Blind Man's Buff with me.

I closed my eyes again, wondering—
Would the moon be there once again
When I opened my eyes? It was—
It's splendid glow on the shimmering sea.

After a hiatus when the moon peeks,
It illuminates the world beautifully:
Happiness after a break when it comes—
Likewise fills my life magnanimously.

Shuvashree Chowdhury

On a Mountain Trail

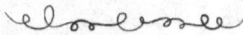

The train chugged along the beaten track
Amidst mountains and lush green trees,
Passing long dark tunnels cut out in rock
To emerge onto sunlit, smoky peaks.

Tiny rivulets it crossed on its slim path
Over narrow, wooden gauge-tracks;
On its course slight waterfalls trickled
Into streams—at which monkeys napped.

Bluebells swayed in the slight, cool breeze—
Amidst pink and yellow wild flowers,
As the fuming engine struggled to push up
A mountainous creaky three line track.

A quaint station came in view from afar
From behind the sprawling tea plantation,
Where amidst tall trees that arrested rain—
The train stopped to water its weary engine.

Quenching its thirst it heartily whistled
As it set off turning the water to steam,
With which it pushed to reach the top—
Looking down at valleys, ravines deep.

As I looked in wonder and enchantment
At nature's picturesque, quaint bounty:
The station guard whistled, waived a red flag
In halting the toy train at scenic Ooty.

An Afternoon Trek

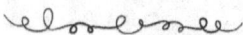

The roads are winding, steep and uphill,
As we trudge on in the afternoon chill;
On either side are valley and hill,
Colourful flowers below pretty windowsills.

Part of the trek we have cloud and wind,
Then there is sun that burns our skin;
Sometimes cars make us swerve to the right—
Left we cross, to catch a breath-taking sight.

Little children holding their mother's hand—
Outside convent gates, in anticipation stand;
Eyes twinkling with pranks they've planned
Since the school bell rang—ending its ban.

At crossroads we stop, to catch our breath,
But more for directions we have to take;
We stop for photographs at picturesque sights—
There are bridges, golf courses, on our stride.

The houses with blooming gardens in sight
Make me wonder about the people inside—
Favoured by nature aren't they fortunate to be
In the lap of mountains with striking scenery!

By now weary from the long uphill walk,
Suddenly from afar we see two armed guards:
They are protecting those training to defend
At the Army Staff College in Wellington.

Shuvashree Chowdhury

A few moments at the war memorial we stand
Then trudge up to the barracks further up;
En route, at suave officers driving past we glance—
Their name badges on blazers—securely fastened.

After pizzas and lemonade at the barrack shop,
Munching homemade chocolates we trek on—
For before dark we have to safely be indoors:
In the hillside room, of our cottage in Coonoor.

A Woman Am I

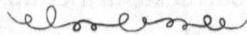

Purple, Orange, Green,
Vermillion, Gold—
Are the myriad colours I'm made up of:
They stand for dignity, compassion,
Enthusiasm; and a determination
Which drives my passionate triumph!

Yet, ever since I was born—
I was solely reared
To be a perfect match
For someone to whom I'd be wed:
So I was dressed with the utmost care
To ensure I was special and rare.

Thus at boarding school I was trained
That I am always to behave—
Tender, obedient, obliging and humane;
I must cross my legs when I sit,
Eat with my mouth shut,
That to burp was a cardinal sin;
Also I was to excuse myself if I cough or sneeze,
Not wear my skirt high above my knee.

Then in college, I was allowed to date
So long as my chastity in line with my life was intact,
While the man I was to marry one day
Could test his virility on all and sundry—
For then would he be man enough to wed me!

Shuvashree Chowdhury

At work, I was amongst all those men
Who were always and compulsively more efficient
For they supposedly had intellect and physical capacity—
Always superior and unequivocally above me!
So even if I was more persistent,
Worked harder to prove my worth over them,
Yet at the end of the month I would go back home
With my pay-packet lighter than those—
Who could share a drink
And a smoke
With another man after work:
In their mirth collectively decide my self-worth!

After I had put into my work all my might,
Proven my worth alright—
I might just get a promotion like the men;
But then—also be termed loose and trite,
For I'd supposedly slept with
The guy who'd been allotted to decide:
For wasn't I pretty, with a body to incite!

Then I'd marry the man
Of my dreams—
Thinking he had a mind of steel,
That he'd be honourable and proud of me;
But then, wasn't it always his
Pride for which I'd watch out?
For where was mine to be found—
It was lost in the shadow of his clout!
So then, I had to be gratified
Like the moon always is—
To shine in reflected glory.

Till when children came along—
They'd expect it's their life I live from then on,
For how can a mother think of anything else—
Isn't she born only to give birth:
Above all cares to bring up children in the world!
But yes, she can only feel proud on giving birth to sons,
Even if they leave their parents and run—
When in old age they need them the most.

A woman am I...
So lifelong I must relegate, must I—
To reflecting the colours of your choice,
In the forms that you callously paint?
Would you not lend me some spotlight—
So I may shine in my own hues,
Thus show you my own true light!

Shuvashree Chowdhury

Walk of Life

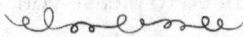

Hand in hand we walked the cobbled roads
Of the small French town, by the coast:
The pretty villas slowly awakening to life—
Their French windows enticing sunlight.

Claret bougainvillea's swaying in the breeze—
Fanned the blue bells dancing on trees;
Tall, pretty women opening their slight doors
Along with their poodles—to walk the road.

Tiny cafés slowly opening their slender gates,
Allowing the fresh coffee aroma to emanate—
From large percolators, through the balustrade
Of rooftops—which well laid tables displayed.

The neat, winding roads led us to the sea shore
Where colourful fishing boats were ready to go;
Dynamic morning joggers rushed passed our fore
As we stood watching the sun now in full glow.

Distinctly, I recalled the time we'd first met—
In your warm eyes I'd seen my search end:
For me—true, lasting love had always meant
Bonding of souls, not mere physical intimacy.

You'd said to me, you loved me for who I am,
Not the pretty sight I am, when I wear makeup.
It's true, what the world sees is not the real me,
But you knew that—you knew my soul already.

Even now when I'm home or alone with you—
No pretence or dress I need to please you:
The façade I wear is for the world to view;
For you, I reserve only 'me'—real and true.

We have now traversed a long eventful way
As we stand by the sea in Pondicherry today:
Knowing we are always meant to stay this way—
Hand-in-hand as one, in life's precarious gait.

Shuvashree Chowdhury

Ashes

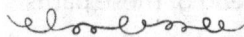

Fire around me everywhere,
The heat intolerable to bear
And yet I cannot feel a thing,
My soul has lost its ability to care.

Covered in ashes from head to toe,
The numerous fires spurting more—
I stand amidst death drenched in rain
Wondering if this is what I live for!

Ashes over me I cannot distinguish—
Which is human, which of material thing?
Human or wooden, ashes are the same:
To turn to ashes then—a lifetime I live!

The drizzle now turns to a heavy shower
Drenching my being to the very core,
Yet on these fires they have no power—
Roaring high over the pyres they've lit.

Below the river Ganges peacefully flows
Washing away ashes the fires have restored;
Men are hurrying around me everywhere
With corpses, guts—for which fires don't care!

Wasn't it this afternoon that I saw her face —
Peaceful and calm in death's embrace:
When bathing and dressing her like a bride,
Grooming her well for the final goodbye.

The narrow, winding lanes as I traversed
I knew what lay at the end of these paths,
Yet I wasn't ready to face the ultimate truth:
My life—is mere ash on the pyre in death!

As I now stand sombrely watching her pyre lit
My heart is numb from all the sights it hit;
My face, eyes, smarting from the thick smoke
Are red—incapable of insulating as my soul.

The Manikarnika Ghat in Benaras, they say
Is the holiest crematorium for Hindus till date—
It frees one from the cycle of Life and Death:
Has given me Moksh from the fear of Death!

Shuvashree Chowdhury

Germanwings Flight 9525

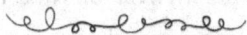

I had to bring us down
No matter what or how;
I needed to belie pain
I felt inside and out!

My anguish as a boulder,
Crushing my ribs asunder;
My soul screaming aloud—
Will someone let me out!

I was drowning in my grief
That ran torrid in my veins;
How could I think of you—
I was gripped by a grue!

You all had faith in me
I would not let you down;
I was guarded by a senior—
He knew his job inside out.

But it wasn't me, please believe
I was only a taciturn spectator,
To a monster overpowering me:
My head—it nurtured his clout!

Please feel a pity for me people,
As I was just as helpless as you:
I was driven by my own demons
While I was the demon to you!

Note: On 24 March 2015, the aircraft, an Airbus A320-211, crashed 100 kilometres (62 mi) north-west of Nice in the French Alps. All 144 passengers and six crew members were killed. The crash was deliberately caused by the co-pilot, Andreas Lubitz, who had previously been treated for suicidal tendencies and declared "unfit to work" by a doctor. Lubitz kept this information from his employer and instead reported for duty.

Shuvashree Chowdhury

A Kerala Rain

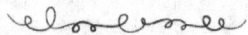

Coir blinds thrash my window sides,
Palm leaves hash the wind in all might;
Coconuts on tall trees violently collide,
Rain lashes the top of the lake I reside.

In the balcony reclining on my armchair,
Rain water drenching my face and thighs—
I look at the canoe static by the lakeside,
It's so uptight—like me it has no respite.

The thunder roars even as the wind whistles—
As sky, woods, lake merge—in grey they hide;
The sight, sound of globs on the lakes surface
Are vigorous as rise of tea-water boiling inside.

Then through the sky there's a shooting light,
The grey cover lifts separating lake from sky;
The woods—shades of green beyond the lake
Is as it was before grey descended on all sides.

My houseboat is safely anchored to the shore
Yet I feel imperilled during turbulent surges:
Shouldn't I then leave an abusive relationship—
Its drifting rattles my core, makes me insecure!

Definitely, Maybe...

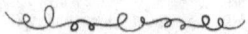

I saw the way you looked at her
With that twinkle in your eyes;
The smile you could not conceal—
As it caught her eyes, also mine.

She smiled astutely, trying to evade me
Yet the gleam in her eyes caught mine;
Rather than let you see my crushed face
I left you both to talk—walked sorely by.

For months now I'd noticed the changes—
A lilt in your voice, a spring in your walk;
The delayed homecomings you justified,
Your phone notifications wouldn't stop.

There'd be outings you both planned
Then invite me to join you as an alibi;
To prove to me that you're just friends
Even a medical emergency you'd defile!

What's worse is you were really nice to me—
Kinder than you had been in a long time:
So I'd be assured you were only true to me
And others were mere cherries on your pie.

I saw you smile by yourself late one night—
You'd not come to bed working overtime,
When I told myself: "Stop living a white lie,
Get on with life—don't ruin it on black lies!"

Shuvashree Chowdhury

Autumn of Our Lives

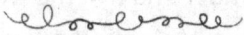

There's so much I want to say to you
But none of which have I been able to;
It is little things in life that truly matter
So nothing big have I ever asked of you.

All effort I make for you with fervour
Is reflection of my deep love for you;
Why then do you dither in showering
The love I know you feel for me too?

There is so much you keep buried inside,
It's me you're in love with never to declare;
The love of your ego you will rather stroke—
Even misunderstandings, my love, to evoke!

You evade the tuneful notes I play for you
While I scavenge yours for what is my due;
I pronounce my love for you in varied ways
Yet you crave all straws women chuck you.

I paint the sky in red, violet I drip on you,
In all the rhymes I sing I envelop you in hue;
The wild green that we paint each other with—
It's because the passion in us still truly rings!

Yet we freeze each other out in our silences
Under which bitter, fuming currents brew;
Now that this high tide is so full of our grief—
With time, a bridge will we ever construe?

You wish I'd become independent and strong—
Allow you space to wander and trot the world:
I'll learn to survive alone, to live without you,
Will you my love carry on, once I'm gone!

Let's throw open our dam of grievances—
So what if we wash each other with refuse?
We'll then cleanse our hearts outpourings:
As egos coalesce—we'll build bridges anew!

Shuvashree Chowdhury

The Break-Up

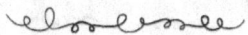

When the phone rang last Sunday,
On the screen your name I viewed;
It constricted my wounded heart in
Rekindling memories I long refused.

Hasn't it been ages since we last met—
From when we parted at your gate?
I'd driven away from your steady gaze
That from my memory never fades.

I softly said "hello," taking your call,
In reply your voice was fixed, cool;
But the feelings between us did ignite
As if a thousand whistles softly blew.

I calmly asked how you're doing in life
But in my heart violet butterflies flew:
In my mind they sailed, perched on you,
Then kissed your lashes, lips gently too!

When you asked me how my life was—
With severity of your baritone diffused,
It blew the lid off your assumed cool
As over the seas our longing brewed.

Speaking insouciantly of those we knew
It was desire for each other we renewed:
You'd missed me, as much as I did you—
Our breakup I ended, saying "I love you."

August Rush

We were sitting by the seaside
After dinner, in the moonlight,
Sipping beer under gallant pines—
As in your hand you took mine.

Rushing to meet us—the waves
Like my heart stopped on track;
The breeze was cool on my spine
But your hand felt warm in mine.

We were meeting for the first time
At a friend's party this August night,
Far from all your friends and mine—
As only in our hearts lyrics thrive.

With the moon and the tide astride
You stroked my long hair very light,
As we talked trivially of our past lives—
What counted was this flash in time.

You turned to look into my wide eyes—
Viewing in them surf rush up the seaside;
I saw in your eyes the surge of a high tide
So yearning of our souls I couldn't hide.

Kissing your lips, as the sea—moonlight,
A connection our souls made that night;
Poetry we're gifted did us further bind—
That we're nature's scions, we surmised.

Shuvashree Chowdhury

Silently we kissed on the face of the surge,
We're August born—a connection firmed;
With time we discovered we're much alike—
Savouring our first kiss with salt of the tide!

Say Something

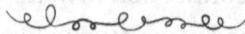

"When I saw you I fell in love, and you smiled because you knew."—William Shakespeare.

I liked the way you looked at me
That evening when we first met,
Across the table, over everybody—
A moment our sights professed.

It was a dinner party for twelve,
All of us meeting the first time;
We'd connected well over wine—
You made an entry in due time.

Alongside me to my right you sat—
A young man between our sights,
Over him you tried to bond with me
But your attempts were all so futile.

Then it was over emails and online
That we connected over a long time,
Thus removing from my perception—
Your arrogance blurring my mind.

Our written words duly thawed the ice
That our first dinner had frozen tight,
Due to facades we both smugly wear
Shielding our hearts broken over time.

The next time, unseen you beheld me
With awe, longing, affectionate pride:

Shuvashree Chowdhury

It unravelled in a photo to my delight
That I may rewind as often as I'd like.

A third time around you gaped at me
As if you were in a state of awed delight:
It was like you'd just seen an apparition
Draped in black – land at your porch!

No one has ever looked at me this way—
With affection, raw desire, rolled in one;
Light of your eyes melted my heart,
Set it off trailing your creative mind.

Now that my molten heart is aglow
By the steady flames from your eyes:
Break your silence and say the words
So my heart doesn't freeze with time!

Divergent Perspectives

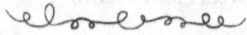

I sowed a tender, unique plant,
Nurtured it with love and care,
Into it I put my time and effort—
It would grow special and rare;
You came along to visit one day:
"The pot's exquisite!" you raved.

I'd decked with care to please you—
My face shone, my hair was styled,
I wore shoes and handbag to match,
The earrings and neckwear were rare:
But it's my dress you complimented—
Overlooking me, as if I wasn't there!

I loved you more than you did yourself,
Did all I could to convey you're the best
But you flashed me your expedient views:
"Jealousy in love is humdrum, out-of-place!"

I worked so hard to shine, to succeed in life—
You saw my sincerity, my competence shine,
But you turned a blind eye as if from the sun
In appreciating the moon—its light reflects!

I communicated but you didn't read my cues,
Leaving me unappreciated, confused always;
Then how was I to love you wholeheartedly
When you solely cared of your own opinions?

Shuvashree Chowdhury

Mustn't we abide, in upholding relationships—
To receive with grace, read what's not explained?
Divergent perspectives can also be communed,
Run parallel on tracks ballasted by compassion.

My Random Moods

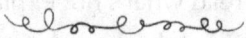

At times I'm so moody and blue,
Also jealous and unforgiving too:
It may have nothing to do with you
But in life, what I've been through.

Sometimes I'll squirm and shriek,
If you dig into my wounded knee—
Purposely poke its scab unhealed:
Then don't blame me for acrimony!

Occasionally I might sulk or weep
When you're happy and carefree:
If you're not sensitive to my needs,
Walk over me in your spiked feet.

With time I will heal, dispel misery,
Cure my jittery heart permanently:
But till then I might act injudiciously
So bear with my moods graciously.

Shuvashree Chowdhury

This Afternoon

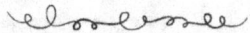

I met a friend—who kissed me gallantly,
His arms around me firm, closer I drew;
But just as he nuzzled my neck, I withdrew—
For it's now I perceived that it wasn't you!

The guy once again held me firm, boldly,
Taking the liberty from being friends long;
But what surprised me was his lust new—
As he said, "A woman I now see in you!"

But what his passion got me to perceive
Was that you're the only man in my view;
I yearn for you as does grass—fresh dew,
Leaving me moist with my desire for you!

In my mind I kiss your eyes, forehead too,
My fingers ache to run your hair through;
You now pull me closer into your groove—
I kiss your lower lip, now your tongue too!

As with firm hands my breasts you grope—
With nimble fingers its firm tips explore;
You gasp as I touch your excitement below,
I kiss your upper lip, with joy we explode!

How can I ever have sex with anyone else,
I only feel you under my skin, in my breath:
Casual sex without love, isn't it unfulfilling—
Now have I to prove that to you, my darling!

An Oyster in the Sand

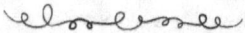

I have nothing anew to say to you—
My soul feels empty, numb and bare,
As all the love I've showered you with
Just wasn't enough to get you to care!

Now that I've given you all I have to give
I can no longer on my heart let you tread,
To allow you further to crush its yearning—
Incapacitating it of loving one who cares.

So go away my love, find your true calling—
Allow me to withstand the suns harsh glare,
Let the waves engulf me body and soul now
Thereby wash away all of you that is yet left.

Surely there's someone there looking for me
With a heart full of love and concern to spare,
That he could not sadly lavish on Her lifelong
For she died young, sorely implanting it there!

I would gladly wash up on him at life's shore,
The waves returning me anew, my soul fresh;
Where he'd pick me tenderly as a gift so rare,
Draw me out from an oyster with loving care.

He would recognise the hand of God in this—
In my washing up on his shore, on golden sand:
Wouldn't my heart he now shelter and cherish,
Acknowledge that it's a pearl valuable and rare!

Shuvashree Chowdhury

As I Taught You to Adore

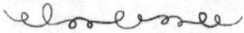

"Forever—is composed of Nows"—Emily Dickinson

I treated you like you were the only one,
You treated me as I was one amongst all,
Yet I gave you all in me I had left to give
As that's the only way I know how to live.

You weren't prepared to drop your ego
While I didn't ever allow it to you show;
I revealed to you, you were at my core,
But you projected I was only at the fore.

You would not support my forays into light
While I was so proud of your every flight;
I restrained from hurting you any way I could
Yet on my bare toes you ensured you stood.

I'd planned every way to brighten your birthday,
To send you a gift, with a dozen red carnations,
But how was I going to have them adorn your life
After your words stung as if I'd poked a Beehive.

Now that we can no longer even communicate,
Living lives in our separate, self-centred ways—
I wish upon you a woman you can celebrate,
As I taught you to adore, teach her to cherish!

Seeking a New Rain

The clouds gently glided
As tender leaves dripped,
Ruffled wet crows quailed,
Mynas crooned transfixed.

A pigeon hopped my balcony
Over the railing, dripping wet;
Streaks of soft lightning tinted
Leaves—in varied green shades.

The sky again turned all grey,
Fresh clouds floated in a haze;
Then came a new torrent of rain—
With the breeze leaves regaled.

I imbibed the varied wet sights
Yet not a drop of rain have I felt,
I'm shielded well from the damp—
Over my senses a canvas I draped.

As early tomorrow I'll go away—
This rain I won't perceive again,
A fresh new life cajoles me now
So a different rain I must crave!

Shuvashree Chowdhury

A Morning Walk: Bekal, Kerala

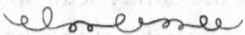

As I strolled the rain-drenched beach
With varied seashells strewing my feet,
They prickled my jute-sandaled heels—
Awakening my intellect to sight and feel.

The waves, they crashed aloud on my right—
Frothy they were, the sea looked as white;
Coconut, palm trees, rustled to my left side,
Birds manifested them—chirping loud, wild.

The sun, didn't yet seem remotely to show
But awaiting it the sky did lay out its glow;
As fissures developed through dark clouds—
Light crept on me slowly, it was dainty now.

Then suddenly there came a burst of light,
As I looked in awe—I was suffused in dawn:
The birds now flew wild, chirped in delight,
Waves crashed noisily—as sun then arrived.

I walked on still, at a steady slow pace now,
Digging my feet into limp, wet, crusty sand,
For I wanted to reach far as sight would go—
Curious to view what lay behind nature's fore!

When suddenly I reached an L shaped curve—
There the beach came to an abrupt, sharp halt;
I walked on further towards the big boulders,
To where—thereupon the sea flowed sideward.

It was here, in flowing through green woods—
An elegant river kissed the dandy sea's lips:
Together they stood in earnest, tight embrace
Even though from them differences emanate.

The sea gurgled playfully, wild waves lashed,
As serene, the river flanked by woods gushed:
I stood over them ingesting their copious spree—
The river blushed, as stroking it was the sea.

Yet they both retained their distinctive charm—
One rough, the other tender: both so in love!
As I walked back leisurely in the soft sunlight,
Nature's lovemaking was intense on my mind.

It's possible to love profusely, be free, distinct,
Two people in love needn't lose individuality:
The sea by now was calm, the birds gone quiet;
Uniqueness in love—from nature I'd surmised!

Shuvashree Chowdhury

By the Ganges

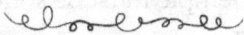

In driving down the winding mud road
An endless yellow carpet as if I strode;
Sun glistened on me through tall trees
Lining the slim avenues I crisscrossed.

Cattle grazed, wiry men with spades ambled,
Tanned women drew water from earthen wells;
Bare-bodied children played in happy abandon
Inside the bare brick houses I curiously gazed.

The yellow carpet swayed in the soft warm breeze
As bountiful, ripe mustard plantations they were;
Though life seemed peaceful and picturesque
Yet tailors, grocers, bazaars, all were present here.

The red patches visible over saffron expanses
Were Rose plantations amidst the mustard fields;
Tall trees above them stood as gallant soldiers,
Shielding Roses from rain and sun – as if ladies,

In this remote village one's life is so well guarded
From the complexities of the stealthy human mind:
Food, clothe, shelter, and love the only wants here
Are interwoven, even if crudely, into life and time.

Sprawling water bodies, amidst thatched huts here
Are fed by the river flowing quietly, peacefully by:
It's five kilometres away from Kanpur I've driven
To the quaint, 'Dhori Ghat' village, by the Ganges.

The loud gong of a bell then went off in the distance,
Pronouncing the river temple must be somewhere near;
The monkeys clamouring over trees that abounded here
As I stood by the river, notified me their feed was near.

The temple priest performed the daily elaborate rituals
As I bowed in complete obeisance with the local people;
The simple folk looked at me with assertive side glances—
For dressed different, was I also amongst God's people?

Staring into the Ganges later, I solemnly wondered—
Why wasn't city life as peaceful and simple as here?
Everything that we need we have aplenty and more,
Yet do we sleep sound, as do simple people here?

Shuvashree Chowdhury

The Thorn

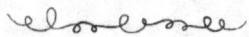

There's a thorn stuck in my heart—
It's seeping my life's blood away:
Yet I allow it inside me to remain
As pulling it out will augment pain.

With every breath, blood it splays—
Blinding me from my true vocation,
But I'll let the thorn inside persist
Till to pull it out courage I may gain.

Then one day our paths cross again—
It's destiny that a mere glimpse we gain
Of each other, even as we strain in vain:
But the thorn in my heart pricks again.

On purpose did you avoid my gaze
Or was it so your heart wouldn't race—
For our time we had with God's grace,
Is lost now to new lives with no trace!

I must pluck the thorn fast as I can
To free my heart, mind, over again:
I'd find a new love faster, wouldn't I—
If only I get rid of that thorn insane!

The Ex-Factor

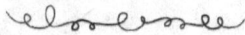

He will remember you fondly
When from his life you've gone;

She might call you if she's blue
When her current love isn't true;

He will think of all you did for him
As peace from his life has slipped;

She might find you most appealing
When with tantrums she is dealing;

He will once again desire only you
When you've no such suicidal whim;

It's after you've walked out their door,
They might see your worth once more;

In lost love's path I'd never walk back:
Nostalgia's fragrant, picking-up pungent!

Shuvashree Chowdhury

The Chennai Deluge

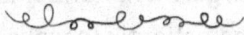

I awoke to sound of a light drizzle that morning,
Looking ahead to a gorgeous and reflective day;
Leaves outside my bedroom window quivered,
Raindrops slapped their tender, coy, shiny face.

Birds were all quiet, crows tucked in their nests,
Cats and dogs wary of rain over the last month;
But I warmed to the last showers of this season,
Awaiting a green teabag infuse into a china cup.

But by afternoon when rain still bashed steadily—
Spouting my balcony, drowning streets in front:
I wished desperately for heaven to stop its play,
Or was it an overflow of its tempestuous wrath!

Beyond evening when the torrent overwhelmed,
Nightlong after it's muscular, wild tirade stomped;
Next morning I awoke wary to yet incessant rain—
A moment's pounding I could no longer endure.

By now rain streamed amok, overflowing rivers,
Running havoc on homes, offices, common lives;
Clogging roads knee-high, marooning walkers,
Strapping families at home, raising a storey high.

The airport turned into a cascade of stranded lives
For those tired, hungry, yet expectant of their fate:
Where could they turn—as tarmac, street's a sea,
Weren't they better huddled inside the terminal!

The army, navy, welfare organisations dispatched
Boats, equipment, food, garments, and humanity,
To rescue those clinging patiently to walls or pillars
Detectible through TV channels, social media posts.

This mayhem rain wrought as I watched in horror—
On television, over filter coffee with my breakfast;
I wondered—could this be the ruins of just a day,
Isn't rain beautiful, nurturing—a nature's marvel!

After I deliberated over the destruction, loss of lives,
The attempt to step out of home once I surrendered;
As I decided to cook a meal with grocery I'd stocked,
To my dismay—the LPG cylinder wouldn't hold up.

I cooked lunch, then dinner, over an electric hotplate
But by now the phone and internet lines, both are down;
Even as I'm trying to stay connected on TV to the world—
The power's off severing all ties: But I still have Hope!

Resilience: For Kathmandu

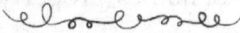

"Sir, Sir, give me money to buy cookies," she cried,
As we ambled by in the chill—approaching twilight;
I couldn't comprehend what it was she had in mind—
Her Nepali tweaked English was distinct from mine.

Construing the puzzlement in my eyes she blurted—
"Give me biscuits ma'am, I'm hungry since last night!"
The teenage girls had come out from asbestos shelters
Or blue tents, by Bhaktapur Durbar Square, I realised.

I shoved all the Nepali currency I had into their hands,
As humbled I was—After shopping Rs.100 is all I had:
Discerning it would not do, to alleviate their raw plight—
An LPG cylinder at Rs. 8000-10000, was bizarre a price!

Yet in the late December chill the girls' smiles did light—
With their sincere gratitude—as if a brazier in my mind:
That for twelve hours a day Kathmandu has no power,
In asbestos cubicles it freezes without blankets all night.

We walked by, miles and miles on the way to our hotel—
As taxis were scarce, fuel rarer, costs at an all-time high;
Only cabs got 5 litres fuel queuing daylong twice a week:
It's four months, with India there's an economic blockade.

Basic medicines are scarce, major surgeries are on hold,
The houseful hospitals cook meagre meals on firewood;
Homes have no electricity, gas, even if groceries to cook—
With children taking 3 biscuits—one per meal, to school.

Isn't it just a few months since the city is raising its head
After mass destruction of homes, property, plenty of lives—
Barely is civilization billeted in tent-camps or tin-shelters:
Tested anew with hunger, cold, manmade strife is unjust!

It was an ordinary day on the date of Christmas last April—
When nearing noon flocks of a variety of birds screeched;
The dogs—both strays and pets, began to howl incessantly
As tremors of an earthquake Kathmandu felt below its feet.

Before humanity yet realised what creatures fussed about—
Snakes slithered out of their hovels, ran amok into homes;
Young people—at best screamed slipping on shaky floors,
As buildings, homes, lives crashed to the precarious ground.

In hours, a day, all heritage sites were a cluster of rubble—
The remnants of Bhaktapur, Patan, Kathmandu Durbar Squares'
Now heavily bolstered by planks, still exhibit natures' fury:
Yet on a frame of stoic resilience, stands poised—vestiges of
humanity!

A Starlit Stage

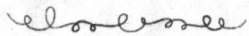

It's a pleasantly cool Calcutta evening
With the January sun on its way down;
As weary boatmen row back to shore—
In the distance I hear strums of a guitar.

I'm sitting by the banks of the Hooghly,
Watching the river serenely flow below;
The sun's giving its ripples an orange glow
In slipping and plunging into its soft folds.

A quiet tranquillity now wraps me snugly
In viewing for long the water's serene flow;
Birds tired of chirping are rushing home
As lights illuminating the bridge turn on.

In the shimmering water I see your shadow,
Faraway notes of a guitar ushers you ashore
To where I'm seated below the strand lights—
Awaiting as on stage, for our roles to enfold.

The last act we played—wasn't it on this shore?
But it feels like such a long, endless time ago!
While I sorely miss your telepathic dialogues,
I have learnt—solo to rehearse both our roles.

In my starlit mind you're real, our opera's true
As the river our audience is in waves of delight—
Writhing in the chilly breeze, like I quiver now
In our last scene—in your passionate embrace.

Magnetic Allure

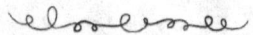

I drove an hour to visit you—
The evening you arrived,
With a gift wrapped bottle
Of Australian red wine.
But to our disappointment
There were guests who arrived
So we sat, politely grappling
With the verbal drawstrings
Of our purse of desires.

We laughed animatedly over
The whisky you served us
With finger chips and chicken fries;
Saving the wine for ourselves:
Though I was already intoxicated by
Your beaming face and throaty voice—
Steeped in the headiness
Of our withheld desires,
In anticipating—
Our long overdue rendezvous.

Sitting alongside me, every time
You looked intensely into my eyes,
I was drawn like a reckless kite
Into the mesh of our magnetic allure—
Dense from mutually yearning vibes
Into weaving a large spider's web:
In which our withheld affections

Shuvashree Chowdhury

As a trapped housefly,
Was struggling
To surrender to our desires.

My Cage is of Gold

You can have your freedom,
But don't seek my devotion;
You can flap your wings wide—
Don't seek access to my trust.

If you don't remain consistent,
My heart might open up again;
It'll permit one who appreciates
And does not seek reckless fun.

Leave my heart's door open—
It'll shut out, so never return;
Just go away to your freedom,
I can choose one who belongs.

I wish you a love that hasn't bars,
One that's yours, his, everyone's:
As freedom seekers I attract aplenty—
My cage is of gold, refracts the sun!

Shuvashree Chowdhury

The Other Woman

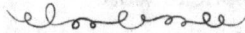

She's always there in my life, what if
I'm a success or failure in my own mind.

I first met her when I was twenty-two,
As she purposefully sauntered into my sight
In a bright pink georgette *Anarkali churidar* suit—
Teamed with black, suede-leather stilettos:
Oh, I thought she was awfully trite!

Plain-featured and dusky,
She first came into my credulous sight
At the theme park's gate, from where
We were to set off on our group outing:
She got off the black sedan car
Driven by my senior in college—
Who for over a year I'd been dating.

He introduced me to her as—'My friend'
But from what I'd heard of her from my sources,
I read much into the fine print of their association:
So in silent protest, stating a family emergency,
Retrieving my soiled pride as if from the gutter nearby—
In view of our large group of friends,
I walked over to my own car
To drive away—oh so coolly, along with a girlfriend!

It was only after dropping my closest friend home
Over cursing my boyfriend's cruelty to the bone,
That I allowed my scorching heart to thaw—

Allowing my smarting eyes to finally flow:
The *kohl* and mauve lipstick I wore
Ruining my white and tender-green *Salwar* suit,
I walked into my room at home, my eyes sore.

Then She returned to my life in a few more years
When I had travelled all the way
To Mumbai from Calcutta, to morally
Support the man who had been courting
Me gallantly on his fortnightly official tours:
He had just lost his coveted job
On charges of sexual harassment,
Which in my youthful naivety
I truly did not comprehend was possible.

Then after landing at the Chattrapati Shivaji airport,
On the drive to my designated hotel,
To my shock he filled me on his 'other woman'—
The one he was to be marrying shortly
Out of a supposed family compulsion!
"She's my sister's best friend—
Who in the circumstances I cannot reject,"
He apologetically and sensitively said:
Just as the realization of his disloyalty on me crashed—
Surging to mind the times I'd helped him shop
Sexy clothes for his sister—over our daylong rendezvous:
Was for this friend, the woman he was now going to wed!
'How could someone cheat me so,' my soul screamed
As if after a car had knocked me down dead
Just outside the airport—hoping we'd never ever met.

Though I was never to see this 'other woman'—
I was wrapped in a pall of shock, swathed in the blood
Oozing from every pore of my being from the sever knock.
I remained silent, merely nodding supportively
As the taxi crept its way to my hotel
Embalming my spirit with the cool January breeze
Of my stupidity—in coming to support this man,
Risking my own shining career
In the same company,
After being warned by my senior boss
Not to stake my own reputation.

The morning after, on the earliest flight back
I wished desperately for it to crash
And spurt my ashes over the Arabian sea:
When a handsome, suave, successful man
Saw my dejected expression on my fresh face,
And to hitch up with me hatched a cool plan.

It was only after a couple of years again,
In the lift of a luxury hotel—
I met a third time over, 'the other woman':
In riding up to a top floor suite
With this suave man I met on that fateful flight
I'd hoped desperately to crash,
Now my boyfriend.
We were on our way to meet his boss from Europe,
After we left the hotel's lounge in a cosy mood
From a few drinks,
Over listening to a live rock band.

A woman along with her girlfriend—
Plain looking as they were
We didn't notice them get off the elevator.
But then, the doors reopened abruptly
To this woman's excited introduction
To my boyfriend as her sister's childhood friend,
With whom she too had supposedly played
At common army postings
Their army officer father's had shared.
Thus igniting their lost friendship, over time.

This childhood friend, then sneaked into my life
Once again as the hated 'other woman'—
Finding her way into my boyfriend's apartment,
To cook him meals like his mother might;
Who living in another city could seldom oblige,
Also due to his extensive travels
Whom he hardly met—much to his disappointment.
So despite my queries on their nostalgic friendship,
I tolerated stories about her that he quipped
With assertions on her being—'just a child.'

Till one late evening, with my close friends
I visited his high-rise apartment
To have her emerge from his bedroom
As if it was her boudoir,
To graciously offer me and my friends tea—
Like I was the guest, she his bride to be!

After a showdown with her and my friends—
In support of me, that crushed my pride,
She wailed and clung to my one-time boyfriend

As a child—like he had always proclaimed,
Even as I silently stomped out:
To shortly learn that this 'other woman' —
Soon beat me to the position as His wife.

But to allay my crushed heart—I was to learn
Decades later in running into him:
She had only desired a trophy husband
Which he had shortly after marrying realized.

It was after I could no longer find in my heart
The depth, to love earnestly as I had several times,
I dated a man, who ironically mistrusted me—
As in his view, I had a 'colourfully tainted' past:
Even though at no time in my life
Had I been disloyal or untrue to any man!
This was after I had myself enlisted my exes for him—
Naive as I was, to wish to share everything of myself
With the man I would spend the rest of my life.

I pacified myself—wasn't his love all mine,
For he was so focussed on me as no man yet;
Absolving his secretly emailing my exes
In spite of my utter embarrassment—
To enquire if I had been true to them:
Thus I patiently tolerated his erratic jealous rages,
Hoping it was a passing phase—over his failed attempts
At catching me disloyal with any other prospective mate;
Thereby I had become assured he was not inclined
To find once again the horrible 'other woman.'

A stiff emotional blow this radically possessive man struck,
When under pressure from my family—he blurted

On arriving hours late, from the time for our registry marriage—
This after 7 years together as an engaged couple
And a couple of inexplicable, failed marriage attempts:
"I must convert to Islam now, to take on another wife again."

After years of justifying my tainted past to him,
Wasn't I crucified and cruelly lambasted, to learn—
I was ultimately the same myself:
The much hated, 'other woman.'
For he had registry married—with no social function yet,
Just before we'd first met and mostly publicly dated,
Thus tarnishing my public and self-image!
It was then I was to further learn to my mortification,
He was seeking, while hiding all of this from me—
A divorce: After which, he and I could wed.

After I had endured all the emotional drama possible—
In a couple of years I married, finally anchored
And safe from the sea of familial matchmakers,
To an eligible bachelor—who in weeks of meeting me
Had decided I was for him the—'perfect woman':
This realisation to him had dawned
Over our multiple long-distance telephonic conversations—
In which I had bared my crushed soul—
Of my learning of the secret divorce application
And awaiting another year to break up a marriage,
Unknowingly becoming the cursed 'other woman.'

But barely a few months after being magnificently wed,
I was awarded for my newly garnered insoluble trust—
For being the coolest, most naive woman he'd met:
By being introduced to perceptively shrewd women

Who were from his profession, and humoured his tastes—
Serially bringing him food they'd cooked as 'good friends.'
Though, mind you—the position of "The Wife"
Was solely and reservedly to be only mine,
Which in his view—I should consider divine!
Though in my by now naive turned convoluted mind
It was my elevated place I wished in my misery—
Upon his every, 'other woman'
Who for years thereon were to come into my life.

Ironically, when I stripped all my reserve and pride
To fall in love so steeply like I've never fallen yet,
As I now feel an inexplicable sublime connection—
Which I have waited to find lifelong;
I am completely robbed of my capability to discern—
Any random woman from 'the other woman':
Like I'm another commonplace neurotic woman—
My experiences having killed the gullible girl that I was,
To have now created one who fears
Her own shadow, as that of the dreadful 'other woman.'

But with sensitivity, love and kindness,
I know someday I will tide over this emotional illness—
That dissolves me painfully as shrapnel might,
From perennial perceived threats of 'the other woman'!

At the Altar of Love

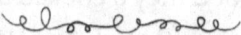

Lonely I strode the woods this morning
Drawn by the urgent chirping of birds,
The sun was still not up in full strength
Though the sky lay out its lighted hearse.

Through the clouds there emanated a chill
That ran down swathing the bristling leaves:
It wrapped my soul as cotton gauze so tight—
Bandaging firmly my bleeding heart and mind.

Insulated, I walked back in time to when we met
Over dinner after a copious amount of red wine;
To when I first looked into your eyes, searching
In their loneliness a home for my own wary heart.

Wasn't it pain that really connected us inexplicably—
Over our mutual attraction through amorous smiles?
Even though we had first come together over words
I splurged in abundance, while you used one a dime!

Over years now we've loved over distance and time,
Connecting hearts over continents, sometimes miles:
As what we kept hand in glove was our soaring minds—
That made love intimately, with a connection divine.

Till one day on my visit to a museum, a message arrived,
Your love for a blue eyed doe you've zealously revived:
To whom you've dedicated my sincerest potions of love—
The ones I wrote for you, scratching my dedicated heart.

Shuvashree Chowdhury

How now, am I going to withdraw from you the deep love
I've showered you with—out of my heartfelt words for long?
When I've learned those words to you were a shallow pond—
Submerged in which you remained in love across its shores!

So now carrying the ashes of my love in my minds urn
I stroll in an aisle of pine wood between pews of trees,
Treading softly as if in church through a choir of birds—
To the altar, past this one way road of unrequited love.

I will place you now in a vault—at the altar of my heart,
The key to which I must carry with me securely, lifelong;
For only this key will open the door to my locked heart—
Allow someone else to find me ready at the altar of love.

Reminiscences

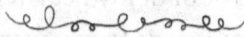

TIME has a beautiful way
Of gradually absorbing
From our hearts the pain of loss—
As cotton gauge
Applied over a wound.

Even as the dull ache ebbs away
With more application
Of the balm called Time,
The scar leaves behind
Its indelible mark and essence:

Translating gently into a slide show
Or at times—random frozen shots
Of cherished memories
Which become more alive
Than the wound might have been.

You then transcend into
A new life of warm, beautiful
Memories, that nothing
But your death can rob you of.

It's as if you're floating
As a new-born
On a large leaf—on the pond
Of everlasting memories.

My Invested Feelings

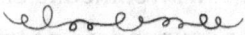

"Love recognizes no barriers. It jumps hurdles, leaps fences,
penetrates walls to arrive at its destination full of hope."

—*Maya Angelou.*

Walking in the drizzle I look for your house,
The traffic is unruly, roads are in puddles:
I ask house guards, passers-by, for directions
Till I finally make it to your grilled front gate,
Through which I see your lined bookshelves.

"Sir has just gone out,' your guard tells me,
So I persuade him to call you to come back—
Since I've tried to reach you in varied ways
After a silent treatment you've doled out to me
To deal with hurt over our accrued differences.

You say you cannot come back to meet me:
'I'm with overseas guests' you evenly assert—
Knowing I might not return ever to your gate
As we live in different towns at extreme ends
And our paths, over work, had by chance met.

My attempts to keep a communication alive
You take for granted, apologies disrespect;
No effort to convey regret for your mistakes—
In nursing your wounded ego above all else:
As my feelings for you to conserve I struggle.

Do I pick my trodden feelings off your stairs—
That in you remain deeply and solely invested?

Fragments | 121

Knowing I'm at times so tempted to recreate
The romance we shared: with someone else—
Who looks like you, has your endearing traits.

Shuvashree Chowdhury

A Way Back Into Love

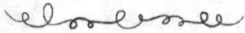

I trusted you with all my heart
After you gave me hope we would last—
That this wasn't just another fling
You'd expect me to brazenly indulge in.

After my heart was worn to shreds
I risked allowing you to sew it up again—
With the light I saw in your kind eyes
And a passion you emanated to my touch.

You also lent wings to my career dreams,
An assurance—with persistence I'll excel:
You said "You have the talents, and potential—
To become anyone who you truly wanted."

How then could you break my deep trust—
Allowing the crystal ball of my heart to collapse?
Crushing with it all our beauteous moments,
Culminating in a Kaleidoscope of painful events!

I know words are not easy for you to utter—
To reflect the melody of your mind and heart,
For you're afraid of displaying vulnerability:
But in lieu of your fear—don't write me off!

Go and find gold lacquer to mend our love,
It's you who callously broke the porcelain vase—
That held the tender blossoms of our hopes:
Kintsugi can fix our vase, beautify its cracks!

A Wedding in the Sky

Dusk approaches
With an orange veil
Of Bridal Illusion tulle,
Shielding ardent Day
Till she's wedded,
From the dark
Amorous
Eyes of Night.

Shuvashree Chowdhury

By the Lake This Morning

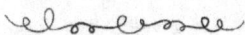

The birds chirped abundantly and aloud
Around the soft ripples of the wood's lake,
As I sat viewing on its moss-green cascade—
The defined silhouettes of trees overhead.

A chilly breeze caressed my just-woken face
As shadows of birds stroked water's surface—
Swathed in soft sun's rays entwined in haze,
Sending shivers up my spine without bane.

Yellow-beaked white birds hopped moodily
On the grassy mud banks—like an audience
Tap dancing in the gallery of a pool-stadium,
Where tender floating leaves danced a ballet.

With a bluebird flying overhead in yellow-red
Awakening, enticing the leaves rhythmic sense:
As a band in a synchronized-swimming recital
They provided a solitary, spiritual experience.

To cleanse my soul of its prohibiting residues—
What I truly need is to tune myself inward:
To delve into my depths and find the reserves
Of strength, hope, a renewed love and peace.

Kanchenjunga Walk: Darjeeling

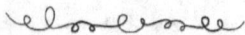

The clouds, they floated up
So amazingly slow,
wrapped the pine trees
In their course;
The sun gleamed
Through thickset groves,
Or was it the orange glow
Of sizzling charcoal?

Amidst steep avenues
As I leisurely strolled,
The Kanchenjunga's tips
White in the sunlight shone;
And though I felt the chill
For long in my bones,
It was at a glimpse of her face
I decidedly froze.

Squatting on the pavement
An iron brazier she fanned—
Over which several cobs of corn baked;
Her fair face now a beet-red
Glistened in its warm haze—
Or was it the glaze of self-assuredness
She brazenly emanated?
It was as if a halo over her she wore
Of optimism—in acceptance of her fight.

Shuvashree Chowdhury

As I walked towards her,
Drawn by her pretty warm smile—
I noticed over the wine-red lips
Her sparkling brown eyes shine;
Then I noticed the thick red vermillion
On the parting of her head:
In his school-uniform, her little boy—
At me—playfully grimaced.

Even as I waited
For my ear of corn to roast,
Another bright face—like the moon
Rising over the hill, came along:
She smiled at the squatting corn-woman,
Both their eyes crinkling ravine deep;
The latter's silver hair shone
Brighter than the mountain peaks.

This approaching woman
Was bent low to retain her balance,
As strapped from her head—behind her
A band of coir rope tarried:
It held two black stroller suitcases,
Also a white tote baggage,
And behind her mountainous bulk—
Strode to a hill-hotel, a young frisky couple.

In awed compassion I then rambled along,
Munching kernels of corn cob;
When suddenly through thick fog what do I see—
Jute basket's strapped behind them on coir ropes,
Two women clambering up towards me:

Both tea pluckers chatted animatedly
About their tough day's work,
Of abusive, rigid supervisors they've reckoned.

A third grill-canopied hangout I came atop,
After crossing two similar ones—
On the L-shaped Kanchenjunga-view walk:
The youth here on their dates often congregate—
Over tea, coffee, corn, peanuts, not much else;
But are dressed as if on the ramp at a fashion show—
Livening the often foggy Darjeeling landscape
With a fashion-sense par excellence!

As I walk on, crunching roasted peanuts now—
The fog shrouds me, or is it the clouds?
Shivering in the chill I dash for shelter
Under the tin stall of a woollen garments seller:
She smiles, bids me to sit, her face is so bright—
Not only from makeup—it's the amber of her warm heart.
Thunder rumbles, as large drops of rain descend, but
I'm sheathed in awe—of the poise, resilience of hill people!

The Twilight Sky

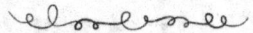

White clouds float over me
In the dusk sky, as if
Swabs of cotton-wool
Embalming my tired mind;
Above a solo bird aims
Majestically for the sky–
Even as a band of coconut
And mango trees rustle
In the heady sea breeze–
To cheer its climb:
Urging me to converse
With the half moon–
Like the lone star
Romancing it tenderly
Under the blanket
Of the cosy grey sky.

London

Through a light drizzle
On the side panes
Of a speeding taxi in black,
I saw you for the first time—
My pretty lady in a sun hat.
Of you, I had dreamt for long
From images formed in my mind,
Out of the novels I'd read
Clutching which—over my heart
I fell asleep feverishly every night.

High over the sidewalks—
With me you seductively strolled along,
The sun bouncing off
Fresh flowers you hold over tall posts
As if your slender, elegant frame
Is hoisting up a classic basket hat:
It was like you were carrying
The enchanting fragrant beauty
Of a summer garden of violet and thyme,
In the cool breeze—fresh and alive.

It was the rush-hour evening traffic
Through which I first stared
At you awestruck, outside Heathrow airport:
My lady, the city of London—
I was instantly besotted by your charm!
You're prettier than images
I'd conjured of you for years—lying awake

Shuvashree Chowdhury

Wrapped in your elegant arms,
Dreaming of visiting you for higher studies
When I'd have the money saved up.

Downstream the Thames

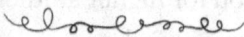

As we glided down the slim river path
Flanked by thick rugs of luxuriant tender grass,
The soft beam of the late evening sun
Warming our faces, under a bridge we crossed.

The flowers swaying in the moist chilly breeze
As varied in colour like the rainbow that peeked;
The moist smell of the woods inhaling deep,
We brushed the light drizzle off our sleeves.

As I lay back on the tartan cushioned plank
In level with the emerald water like a raft—
I looked to my right and what do I see:
A little duck struggling to keep pace with me!

I closed my eyes to seal in the sublime beauty—
Upon all my senses it showered bountifully:
On opening my satiated eyes what should I see—
A group of ducks was floating alongside me!

Under a pretty bridge when again we crossed—
The blue-eyed punt girl in local accent said to us:
"Magdalene Bridge—off the river Cherwell it is,
From Oxfordshire we're punting downstream."

Shuvashree Chowdhury

Our Worldview

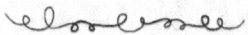

"The universe is wider than our views of it."—Henry David Thoreu.

We tend to narrow the universe
with our constricted
Thinking and close minded
Perspectives, don't we?

We must trash anything
We do not find familiar,
In our classified cushy worlds—
With our limited vision!

Then we must go ahead, make
A mockery of anything that grows
Outside our rose tinted vials—
While cramming ourselves into it.

It is in oblivion then, we now see
The world outside of the shaded
Vial—in a different colour
From what actually it is!

At the Cinema Last Evening

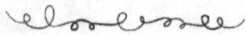

I walked into the multiplex cinema
Through a metal detector at the door:
My handbag they checked at random
As trailing me a lengthy queue strode.

I turned around, awaiting my friend—
When a silver haired couple trod inside:
They didn't get past the check as I had
As they held on to a packet of fried snack.

The man was clad in a faded cotton *lungi*,
High above wrinkled ankles, the lady wore—
A sari, tatty as the age their faces bore:
But in childlike excitement their eyes shone.

As I watched, a manager briskly strode up,
With a walky-talky, an upright stern look in tow:
He repeated what they'd been told before—
The snacks in cellophane they'd have to forgo.

The couple blushed, conscious of the crowd
As they asked the manager why this was so:
I stared at their deflated faces, their eyes aglow—
Abashed I shifted my gaze firmly to the floor.

But the manager shook his head vehemently,
Insisting they could not go past this porch,
To their first row seats at ten rupees a show:
Though this packet doubtless cost them more!

Shuvashree Chowdhury

Looking at me shyly, they walked out the door
With dejected eyes, smiles in place, amore:
They would snack together foregoing this show
At the first row, hearing munches from back rows.

I stood rooted at the glare of humanity so stark—
Then related it to my friend viewing me in shock:
My face was contorted in remorse as I'd not implored
To buy them food—in lieu of their dignity indoors.

As the movie rolled out at length, all I thought I saw—
Was the back of the couple's heads pulsating in mirth,
In validating a system that deprived them of a film show—
By pricing tickets so low, yet of their delight it ignored!

Note: As per the government directive, every theatre in Tamil Nadu
reserves a row of seats, usually the first, costing only Rs.10 a ticket.

My Possessive Pride: The Jallikattu Uprising in Tamil Nadu

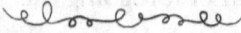

It's my culture, it's my pride;
Don't deny me my right—
To upkeep what for generations
Has been my birthright!
In my need to assert my identity,
I must fight all conceivable might—
That in my sentiment does not align.

But what of the innocent creatures I malign—
In my firm belief it is justly their plight:
In my rationalization, I'm allowing them a mate
As reward for their uncharacteristic defensive run.
So what if they're trampling my own kin, splashing blood—
Don't I love these creatures I garland, as my blood kin?

Just as, I love 'My' wife—so what if I crush her profile;
'My' son, must he not follow in my chosen stride—
Failing which from my inheritance I will him deprive!
'The' daughter had better not wed hurting my pride
For I would rather kill her if I must—before she is a bride.
As for 'My' husband, all his breathing time is solely mine!

In that case, how can 'My' pet dog crave beef or pork—
Aren't these banned by my religious conventions?
Can't I give him chicken—his instinctive preference:
But no, 'I'm' his lord and master, and 'My' law abides,
Am I and 'My' household not purely vegan!

Shuvashree Chowdhury

So people, allow me to upkeep my pride
Or I will scurry up a tumultuous revolution:
It's peaceful—so it's justified!
With my agitation, you will be forced
To bend to the Cause of my brittle pride—
Even if it turns violent overnight!
So what if my exemplary, law abiding homeland,
To my indignity, by the world is renamed, Volatile!

But 'My' Lord, please don't challenge my solemnity
Or my devout behaviour and pious style:
You're apprised of my need to protect my pride
That you threaten to rob me of, from time to time!
Let the ownership of those I love, also worship—
Whether man or beast, be my birthright:
Don't question my intentions—they're after all kind!

Note: In January 2017, thousands of protesters, especially the youth, took to the streets and sat in silent agitation at the Marina beach in Chennai, to demand the removal of the ban imposed by the Supreme court in 2014, on the traditional bull taming sport of Jallikattu, conducted during the harvest season of Pongal. Amidst reports that Jallikattu was still being organised in Tamil Nadu despite a Supreme Court stay on it, animal rights activists requested the Centre to impose President's Rule in the state, for "deliberate and malicious non-implementation" of the apex court decision. The campaigning turned rowdy after the police tried to use force to disperse the crowds.

The Baton of Power

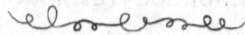

I've lived in her charismatic shadow all my life,
Guarding her halo—of beauty, fame, and power;
I bided my time to step on the political stage—
Coaching myself, under an uninterested cover.

The greenroom, provided a close up view of the drama,
Lending me ample light to nurture my own exposure:
As if my life's film I was developing in the dark room,
I came into public light when her life's show was over.

My dreams and ambitions I kept tightly wrapped,
In a solid blanket—of a stoic, silent demeanour:
Even as I fanned my families lofty aspirations
With resolute determination, sans a nervous tremor.

The loyal hearts of Tamil Nadu scorned at me
For scheming against their beloved Chief—Jayalalithaa:
They didn't know, I Sasikala, was her shadow so long—
So someday my face and fame might precede her in posters.

People, why didn't someone tell me—ambition, grit, willpower
Aren't adequate propellers in this murderous race for power:
If education, experience, wisdom haven't been your preceptors—
A solid baton of trust, is vital, to run a race you've hankered!

Note: From lying low for many years under the shadow of former
Tamil Nadu Chief Minister—Jayalalithaa, to hogging the limelight at
her funeral on 6th December 2017, in a new avatar as 'Chinnamma',
controversies and bribery allegations continued to haunt V.K. Sasikala,

Shuvashree Chowdhury

leading to tremendous opposition from various factions. As Jayalalithaa had no biological heir or a declared political successor and with her party—AIADMK's organisation/ideological engine solely driven by a deep loyalty to 'Amma (Mother)' as Jayalalithaa was respectfully called, her demise opened up an overt power struggle for the top post in Tamil Nadu.

This Morning at Five: Thimpu, Bhutan

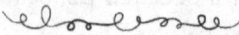

The monastery on the hilltop,
Shrouded in a haze of fog—
Is nestled amid tall Ferns
That hood its privacy from the world.

I awake again viewing its silhouette
From my bed, this morning at five—
Watching the fog lift off its golden lining so high,
As my eyes adjust to light streaking outside.

Monks—male and female, in maroon habits
Become visible, as I sit up on my bed cross-legged:
Their shaven heads float into view as do worshippers—
Fingering prayer beads, briskly climbing steep steps.

Chirping of a variety of birds permeate my senses—
Yet I can hear each one distinctly well
Through the incessant barking of a Lhasa, other dogs nearby:
My soul's harmonious sanctum no clamour can now defy!

A Spiritual Hike: To Taktsang (Tiger's Nest) Monastery

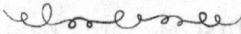

It was at twelve-thirty of a late June day—
With light showers through the sun's soft rays,
We set out to climb on foot—the narrow, steep
Mountainous trail at Paro's heart:
Driving past her white-pebble lined arterial river Pachu
That flows eloquently through her rustic
Frame, then is flanked by flower-lined cottages
And bridges—on uphill picturesque paths.

After peering over numerous handicraft
Stalls displaying mostly stone-jewellery
Of every colour and form, under the wood
And tin canopied shopping enclave,
We crossed it to step on to the rarely used trail:
Foregoing the broader, safer, beaten track
People climb on colourfully dressed ponies—
Or trudge uphill—to reach the fog draped
Mysterious cliff at 3,120 ft. above sea level:
That cradling Bhutan's holiest monastery,
Majestically beckons one to its amorous heart.

Wanting to save on time, we've risked
A tedious climb, as our group of six—
Of four local Bhutanese youth, comprise:
Who'll take us up in two hours, by a short-cut
Instead of the ascertained three to four hours;
Reaching us well before the monastery gates
Close at five—barring us from the peace
Of the sanctum we seek—en route relieving our sins

As is popularly believed, through the toil
Of the wearying, challenging, dreary climb.

I was excited over the first few yards, by
The picturesque view of dainty bridges, tiny stupas,
Also varied Rhododendron—around hill-water crests
From which by the hand-full we thirstily drank;
Till a colourfully saddled, rider-less horse
Came gawkily strutting downhill:
With his coir reins entangling in his front hoof —
He ensnared my attention,
Wilting my heart with his helpless plight,
To trot off straddling my steady breath—
Leaving me to gasp terminally
The rest of the precipitous climb;
A native girl sturdily tugging me up thereon.

After a three hour climb and a half-hour halt
In steady drizzle—once the Tiger's Nest white stone walls
And golden tiered roofs are visible,
Our Bhutanese friends
Stop to drape their *Gho* and *Kira*—their traditional dress,
In respect: As I bid my last dash of strength to press on,
Though my breath soon threatens to desist
On the final 350 steep, stone steps—on which
The air is so sharply thin and crisp,
I gasp ominously— alarmed it's my Death Whistle!

Once inside the temple, as if floating between life
And death, I bow my head to the floor to Guru Rinpoche—
The patron sage, and his manifestations:
Till I interpret 'Nirvana'— viewing the mystical glow
On Buddha's striking golden face!

After the Rain

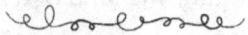

I can still hear the rain pattering
On red and green ridged tin rooftops—
Against silhouettes of mountainous forests
In varied lush tones of emerald.

Grey clouds are soaring skyward,
As fog steadily descends:
Between clouds and fog
A magnificent light bursts forth—
Illuminating 'the land of thunder dragons.'

Ink-blue sky peeps intermittently below grey clouds,
Right through the splendid light:
Even as fog creates a halo, after the rain stops—
Over the stupa's many tier ed golden roofs.

A man or two in tartan brown and black *Gho*
Have descended onto the rain washed streets;
As a woman in a purple and white silk *Kira*
Walks past my window, placing her feet cautiously—
As do cars drive now, ascending a light-swathed wet valley.

In the distance—I see grey peaks, white peaks
That are etched out in thick smog,
As clouds through them hop in and out in turns—
As if characters playing their part for an audience.

The stage of green woods is irradiated as if by Arc light,
While through fog, mud-tracks are visible

On hills in the backdrop:
As ageless hearts in Bhutan, 'the land of happiness'—
Illumined by spirituality, are unfazed by anguished deluges!

Shuvashree Chowdhury

Solitary Enchantment

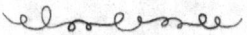

My cottage in the green woods is
Made of mud and pine wood, it's
Nestled in the crook of tall ferns
And a variety of thick green bush.

To the right side is a clearing in
The woods—drops sharply into a
Deep ravine, over which sunlight
Creeping uphill stealthily, sneaks
Past my ethnic Bhutanese—blue
And red blinds, waking me at five.

I am now sitting at my doorstep—
The topmost of five stone-stairs,
Where the cool breeze is floating
With haze, and caressing my face.

I listen intently to piercing whistles—
Intermittently from atop the Fern
And Cypress, amid diverse chirping
Of mixt birds hidden from my sight:
Perhaps sitting on branches astride—
Noting, envying my solitary delight!

Stealing a Slice of Sunshine

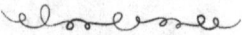

I'm walking downhill the boulevard—
With picturesque sights at every verge,
Through which I see rhododendrons
And roses at doors and windows of cottages:
With the backdrop of a peeking, pristine blue sky
Through hills, over which clouds playfully pry.

Even as I stand in awe at every other hedge-gate
To steal an eyeful of nature's abundance—
Thimphu in the 'land of happiness' is blessed with;
A few furry dogs invariably come barking up at me:
They merely sniff around, and quietly watch me—
Even as I steal a bit of the setting sunshine.

I stroll on with an eyeful of pictographic joy, collected
As if alms at a doorstep—of a handful of rye;
My soul, is as that of a solitary wandering monk's
As it's floating light in the cool misty sky:
For in my mind's eye, I'm collecting gratuitous sights—
Carrying them along in my heart's inflated pouch.

Cars floating uphill I deftly dodge in my photographic sight—
As two boys dribbling a football becomes primary highlight;
After I walk by, satiated with their polite innocence
Infused with a woody aroma and the chill, in soft sunlight:
My heart is full of generous alms of sights I've imbibed—
To carry back to my world, as a perfume, titled—'Sublime.'

Shuvashree Chowdhury

The Path I Built

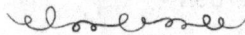

In my search for light
That will illuminate my life;
Also give me peace and quiet
And a purpose that overrides strife—
I dreamt of a garden path
Flowing over a stream of views
I have channelled lifelong:
Out of many an uphill walk
At varied jobs—
In a quest for the meaning
Of my birth.

Little did I envision then,
The path I'd dreamt of and chosen—
Was the most arduous yet:
As it was guarded
By overzealous gardeners,
Who only grew flowers
They could sell easily and well;
Whereas I nurtured my garden
With all good intent,
To nourish and keep people
Inherently well.

After many a crushing defeat
To walk a mercantile literary trail,
As I was almost ready to give up:
I decided to build my own unique path
Which would take people

Over a stream of thoughts and words,
To a well manicured garden—
Where they could rest
Their wearied minds;
Recoup their inherent strength
To face the dilemmas of life.

Shuvashree Chowdhury

Letting Go

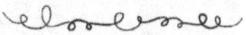

Before me now the river Ganges peacefully flows,
Its green ripples frothing over white cobbled stone;
Grazing boulders it glides with no perceptible force—
Yet it flushes my heart of all its obstinate toxic woes.

I sit for hours engrossed in the waters rhythmic flow—
As to a classical raga by the eloquent strums of a Sitar:
With my back basking in the sun's late morning glow
I'm anointed by a cool breeze swathing the holy flow.

As my soul is liberated from all debilitating worldly ties—
I'm one with my creator, no fear of rejection I now nurse;
I feel free of a lifelong search for inherent self-projection
As palms full of water I offer Ganges, thrice in obeisance.

Unable to leave yet, I slowly walk close to the water's edge—
For to this holy current I've developed a deep attachment:
In filling the void—a crutch for my soul I've now created,
I still need time to be free from craving worldly affections!